Charges may be payable on books overdue at public libraries. This book is due for return by the last date shown but if not required by another reader may be renewed – ask at the library, or if you have a pin number, telephone 0845 6022815 or renew online.

Raintree is an imprint of Capstone Global Library Limited, a company incorporated in England and Wales having its registered office at 264 Banbury Road, Oxford, OX2 7DY – Registered company number: 6695582

www.raintree.co.uk
myorders@raintree.co.uk

Edited by Gina Kammer
Designed by Julie Peters
Original illustrations © Capstone Global Library Limited 2020
Picture research by Morgan Walters
Production by Kathy McColley
Originated by Capstone Global Library Ltd
Printed and bound in India

ISBN: 978 1 4747 8583 9 (hardback)
ISBN: 978 1 4747 8589 1 (paperback)

British Library Cataloguing in Publication Data
A full catalogue record for this book is available from the British Library.

Acknowledgements
We would like to thank the following for permission to reproduce photographs: Getty Images: Alamy: Avalon/Photoshot License, top 13, Doug Perrine, bottom 12; Getty Images: David Doubilet, bottom 18; Newscom: Credit Paulo de Oliveira/NHPA/Avalon.red, bottom 26; Science Source: Jessica Wilson, (map) 14; Shutterstock: Achimdiver, 28, Adriana Margarita Larios Arellano, top 22, Andrei Minsk, (maps) 9, Borisoff, (sea) Cover, Dale Warren, top 7, Damsea, bottom 16, divedog, (seaweed) design element, Dudarev Mikhail, top 19, fluke samed, bottom 24, HelenField, (earth) bottom 5, Iakov Kalinin, (beach) design element, khwanchai, bottom 20, Kitnha, (map) middle 5, Kondratuk Aleksei, bottom 10, Krzysztof Bargiel, (fish) design element, Lickomicko, (map) 22, Milos Kontic, (diver) Cover, NoPainNoGain, bottom 8, Paul Rawlingson, top 17, PHOTO JUNCTION, (blue water) design element, Pro_Vector, (map) 27, sergemi, bottom right 4, stihii, bottom 21, superjoseph, middle 15, TierneyMJ, 23, touchoforange, top 11, Vecton, bottom 6, Vitaly Korovin, (reef) design element, Vladislav Gajic, 29, vovan, (beach wave) design element, ZoranOrcik, top 25

Every effort has been made to contact copyright holders of material reproduced in this book. Any omissions will be rectified in subsequent printings if notice is given to the publisher.

All the internet addresses (URLs) given in this book were valid at the time of going to press. However, due to the dynamic nature of the internet, some addresses may have changed, or sites may have changed or ceased to exist since publication. While the author and publisher regret any inconvenience this may cause readers, no responsibility for any such changes can be accepted by either the author or the publisher

CONTENTS

THE LARGEST HABITAT ON EARTH

Imagine life on Earth without water. An empty, desert-like land stretches out before you. Dead, dry. Could you live in such a world? Probably not.

Today, almost all life on Earth relies on water. Without it, humans wouldn't exist. Throughout our history, people have lived near water. We rely on it for drinking, washing and watering crops. Water is what the five main habitats – **aquatic**, forest, desert, tundra and grassland – have in common. Habitats are large areas with a particular type of climate, plants and animals.

Coral reef

aquatic to do with water

The two major aquatic habitats are the marine habitat and the freshwater habitat. The marine habitat can be broken down into three types: oceans, coral reefs and **estuaries**. It is by far the largest habitat in the world because it includes the five main oceans: the Pacific, Atlantic, Indian, Arctic and Southern. The marine habitat also includes seas and tidal areas.

Bering Sea

Arctic Ocean

Mediterranean Sea

Pacific Ocean

Atlantic Ocean

South China Sea

Caribbean Sea

Indian Ocean

Southern Ocean

FACT
Water makes up the largest part of Earth, covering more than 70 per cent of the planet's surface. From space, Earth looks like a water world.

estuary mouth of a large river, where the saltwater from an ocean or sea meets the fresh water

The marine habitat is different from the freshwater habitat because of its water. Marine water contains salt. This salt comes from rocks on land that have **eroded** into the oceans and seas. The water later evaporates and returns to land as fresh water. This process is part of the water cycle. All plants and animals on the planet get most of their fresh water from the saltwater of the marine habitat.

The marine habitat provides more than just fresh water. We often think the oxygen we breathe comes mainly from trees. But plants that live in oceans provide much more of Earth's oxygen.

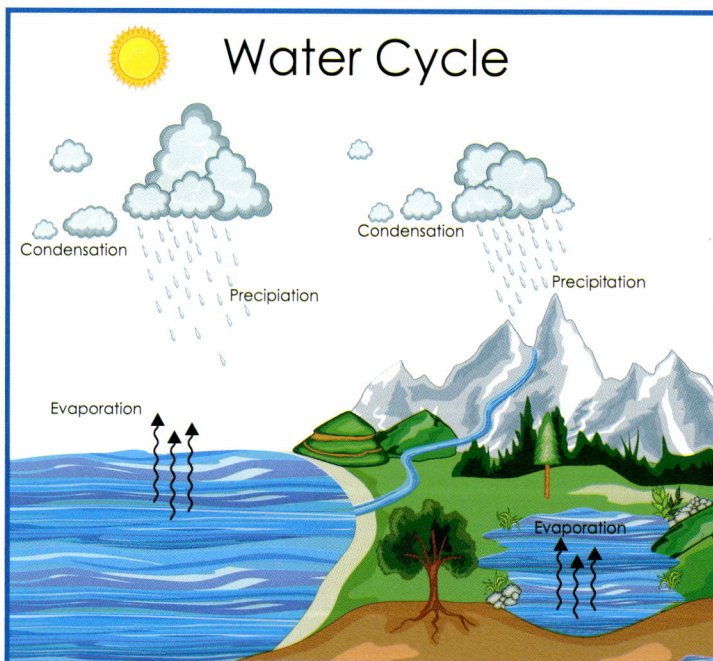

Water Cycle

Condensation

Condensation

Precipiation

Precipitation

Evaporation

Evaporation

Water that evaporates from the ocean is fresh water. It does not include the ocean's salt. Air currents raise the moisture where it condenses into clouds. From the clouds, it falls back to Earth as precipitation, such as in rain or snow. Some of this water flows back to the ocean. The cycle starts again.

erode gradually wear away

Prawns and fish are caught by fishermen in Cambodia to sell at market.

Today almost half the world's population lives within 100 kilometres of marine coasts. Why? At first, people moved or migrated in order to be closer to the oceans as a source of food. Later, when trading routes opened up, estuaries and river mouths served as easy ways to transport goods. Ports and harbours provided access for ships to dock and unload and load supplies. The marine habitat continues to give people fresh air and water. It also remains a way of transportation and a precious source of food. Seafood is important to many countries for both food and money. Ocean views and seaside activities also attract people to the marine habitat.

OCEANS: THE BIG BLUE

Oceans are the largest parts of the marine habitat, making up much of Earth's surface. Oceans are so massive and deep that they can be separated into five zones: sunlight, twilight, midnight, the abyss and the trenches. Each zone has many species. These plants and animals have adapted to their unique environments. The oceans contain the greatest variety of species on the planet.

ocean surface - 0 ft (0 m)

sunlight zone
660 ft (200 m)

twilight zone
3,281 ft (1,000 m)

midnight zone
13,123 ft (4,000 m)

abyssal zone
19,685 ft (6,000 m)

the trenches

SUNLIGHT ZONE

The sunlight zone stretches from the ocean's surface to about 200 metres below. This zone has the most light. The light allows marine plants such as seaweed to grow. Many marine animals feed on **phytoplankton** and smaller fish. Most ocean fish, including sharks and rays, live in this zone. The animals have adapted to use their eyes to hunt prey or avoid predators.

FACT

The Pacific Ocean is the largest ocean in the world. It covers almost one-third of the entire surface of Earth! The Atlantic Ocean is the second-largest ocean. It's a little more than half the size of the Pacific Ocean.

phytoplankton mainly single-celled plants that live in water and use sunlight and carbon dioxide to make food and oxygen by photosynthesis

TWILIGHT ZONE

The twilight zone is directly below the sunlight zone, reaching down to 1,000 m. Light is much fainter here than it is above. There is enough light to see during the day but not enough for plants to grow. Larger marine animals such as whales and giant squid dive to these depths to feed on prey. Many fish have large eyes to absorb as much of the dim light as possible. In this zone, some fish glow with **bioluminescence**.

bioluminescence production of light by a living organism

Giant squid

MIDNIGHT ZONE

The midnight zone descends into darkness up to 4,000 metres down. Fish create their own light using their bodies through bioluminescence. The great pressure of the water in this zone would crush an unprotected human. But a squid, for example, can survive because its body contains no air. There are no "gaps" in its body to be crushed. Many fish have soft bodies to survive the water pressure. Their slimy skin has adapted to protect them from the cold. A few have large eyes that are 100 times more sensitive to light than those of a human. Others have no eyes at all. They use senses such as smell to find their way around.

ABYSSAL ZONE

The abyssal zone is deep, dark and close to freezing. There is no light at all, and fewer animals live at these crushing depths up to 6,000 metres below the surface. The animals found here are often invertebrates, which have no backbone, such as tiny squid. Their grey or black bodies are an adaptation to the darkness. This camouflage allows them to blend in with their surroundings. Many have large jaws to sift through the sand of the ocean floor. Most of the ocean floor is found in this zone.

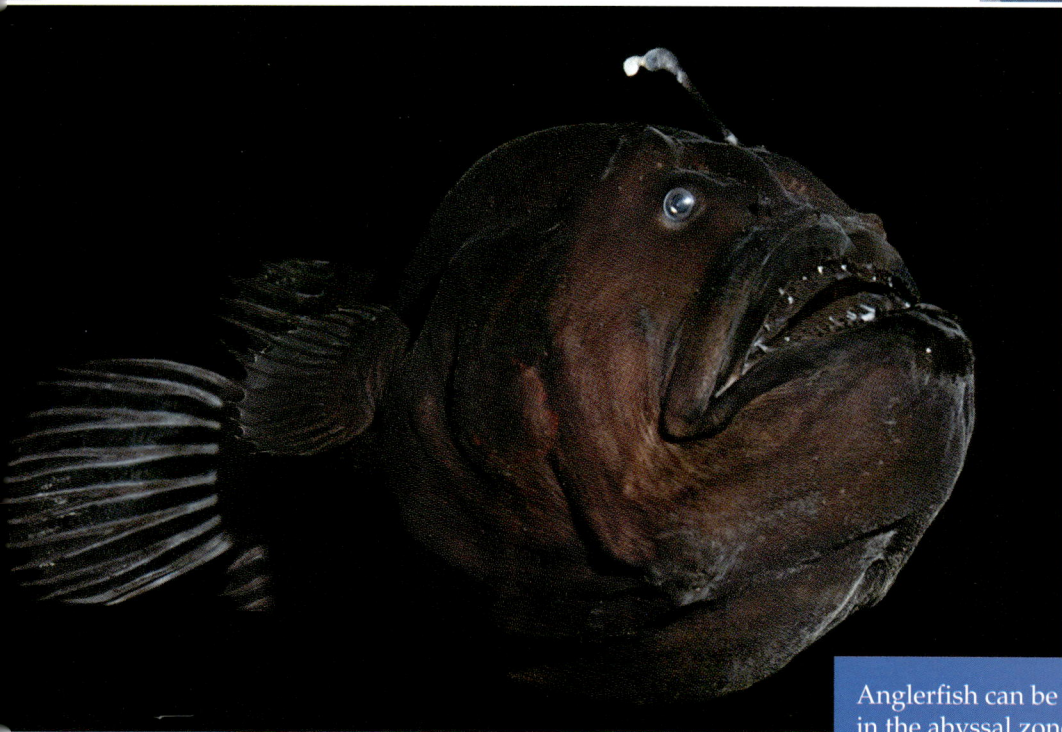

Anglerfish can be found in the abyssal zone.

THE TRENCHES

The trenches zone is the deepest part of the ocean, below 6,000 metres. The water is near freezing. The weight of the water is the same as 48 Boeing 747 aeroplanes sitting on you. Despite this, life is still found here. Fish move slowly to conserve energy and need very little oxygen. Soft-shelled **crustaceans** called amphipods live here. They look like large fleas. Trench animals have adaptations similar to those of animals in the zones above, such as having no air in their bodies. Most use bioluminescence to attract food or for disguise.

crustacean animal with a hard outer skeleton, including crabs, lobsters, crayfish, prawns and barnacles

CORAL REEFS: ᴬ SAFE HOME

Coral reefs are part of the marine habitat. They form some of the most beautiful places on the planet. Coral reefs are found in warm, shallow water. They often act as barriers to nearby land. They can surround the edges of continents and islands. There are three main types of coral reefs: fringing reefs, barrier reefs and atolls. Fringing reefs are close to shore and found in shallow water. Barrier reefs are further out and are in deeper water. Atolls are rings of coral that surround a lagoon. They look like islands.

■ reefs around the world

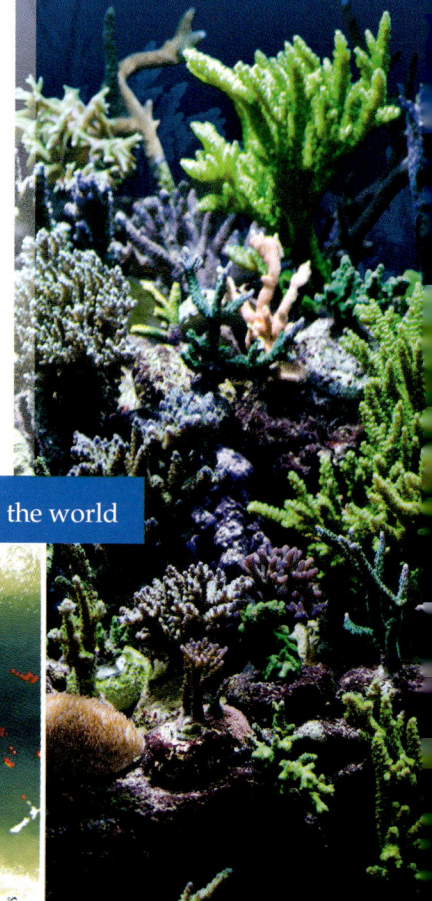

A coral reef is made from **coral polyps**, which are animals, not plants. When you remove coral from the water, that part is the hard shell of the polyp. A cluster of polyps growing together gives reefs their shape. They provide a home, shelter and protection for the many sea creatures that live in the reef.

FACT

Large reefs such as the Great Barrier Reef in Australia are between 5,000 and 10,000 years old! That reef is made up of 2,900 smaller reefs. It covers about 2,575 km, 900 islands and is one of the most visited reefs in the world.

coral polyp tiny organism that has a hard limestone skeleton; the skeletons form the structure of coral reefs

Thousands of sea life species call coral reefs home. These include **microorganisms**, plankton, algae, seaweed, fish, jellyfish, sea anemones, sea urchins, octopus and starfish. In fact, coral reefs provide homes to almost a quarter of all marine life. Many fish species use coral reefs as nurseries for their young. Animals that live in coral reefs, both predators and their prey, are often masters of camouflage. They have adapted to the region and blend in with the coral, rock and sand that surround them.

A Suenson's brittle star blends in on a branching fire coral.

Strong waves wear down coastlines.

The coral reef plays an important role in the survival of our planet. Coral reefs protect coastlines from erosion by acting as barriers to waves and storms. They provide many resources that a marine **ecosystem** needs.

FACT
There are more types of fish in a hectare of coral reef than there are bird species in the whole of North America!

ecosystem system of living and non-living things in an environment
microorganism tiny organism, usually a bacterium, virus or fungus

Coral reefs provide many benefits for humans, such as fish for food. In countries such as Indonesia and Papua New Guinea, fishing villages are often located near coral reefs. Because they rely on the coral reefs for survival, people in these fishing villages have learned to adapt or change with their environment. For example, some villages allow fishing for a few years and then close the fishing grounds for nine months. Others close their coral reefs to fishing most of the time and then do a lot of fishing at once. This helps fish numbers increase and the fish themselves to grow bigger.

A father and son fish in the healthy reefs of Papua New Guinea.

Fishing is an important source of money and food for people on the coasts of Sri Lanka.

Reefs are also important to the worldwide fishing industry. Smaller fish species breed and grow in reefs. They are the food supply for large predator fish such as tuna. People in the worldwide fishing industry hunt these large fish species.

FACT

Coral reefs can help people live longer! Scientists have found that parts of coral reefs can be used to make medicines to treat cancer and other illnesses.

ESTUARIES: A PLACE TO GROW

Estuaries are another type of marine habitat. In these places, freshwater streams and rivers meet and mix with the saltwater ocean or sea. Lagoons, river mouths, inlets and harbours are also estuaries. Some are always open to the sea, but others are only flushed with seawater during storms. Estuaries keep the water clean and clear by filtering the **sediment**. Estuaries are shaped by tides and the weather. Reefs, islands or areas of mud and sand help protect some estuaries.

Aerial view of a river meeting the ocean

These areas of mixed water create a unique ecosystem that is home to many types of animals and plants. Plants such as algae, seaweed, marsh grasses and mangrove trees grow well in estuaries. Animals living here include worms, oysters, crabs and water birds. Other species pass through estuaries during their migrations. A good example is the salmon, which migrates from the sea to rivers to lay its eggs. Once born, the young fish migrate back to the sea. Many **migratory** birds use estuaries to rest and eat before continuing their journeys.

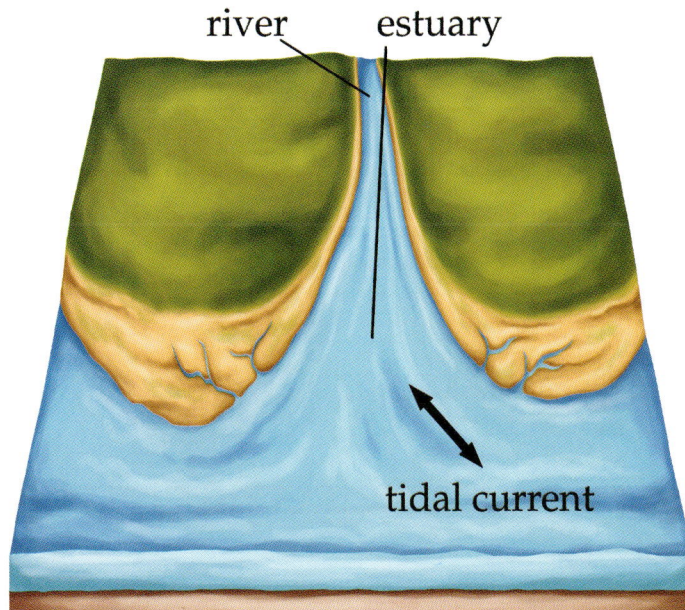

river   estuary

tidal current

migratory having a way of life involving regular travel, such as animals that usually move great distances to find food sources
sediment sand, mud and other particles produced as a result of weathering

Animals living in estuaries are also important sources of food for humans. People harvest shellfish such as mussels, oysters, crabs and prawns. Bottom-feeding fish such as flounder are common.

Men fish with a net in an estuary in Mexico.

Estimated Population - 2014

- 0 - 40,000
- 40,001 - 80,000
- 80,001 - 120,000
- 120,001 - 160,000
- 160,001 - 200,000
- 200,001 - 240,000
- 240,001 - 280,000
- > 280,000

The Chesapeake Bay on the east coast of the USA is the largest estuary in the United States. Over 18.2 million people live in the region.

Many villages were built near estuaries because of the rich food source estuaries provide. The Maori people of New Zealand, for instance, have always valued estuaries and have learned to treat these areas with respect. They limit fishing in certain areas. In other areas, they only take what is needed and do not fish during breeding season. Fishing nets in some parts are only allowed to be used once a year.

New York City is located on the Hudson River Estuary.

FACT

Towns or cities are usually located near estuaries because of the abundant food supply. Estuaries provide ways to transport goods and people. However, this function also puts estuaries at risk from pollution such as sewage and waste.

HUMANS AND WATER

While people greatly value and benefit from the marine habitat, they are also its greatest threat. By polluting and overfishing the marine habitat, humans have affected every part of this complex ecosystem.

Oil is one of our most used and useful energy resources. However, locating and extracting oil creates some risks for the marine habitat. Oil is often located below the sea floor. During an oil spill or accident, sea creatures either become covered in oil or swallow it. Oil also affects the food chain by **contaminating** all food sources. This contamination affects humans as well, because many people rely on seafood for survival.

Crabs on a beach are covered in oil.

A fisherman pulls fish out of the water with a net.

Fishing in developed countries has had a severe impact on the marine habitat. Fish numbers have halved since 1970 and are now the lowest they've ever been. Numbers of some types of fish have decreased by 75 per cent. In addition to overfishing, modern fishing methods can harm the habitat. Massive fishing boats drag huge fishing nets behind them. The boats and nets damage and destroy marine habitats on the sea floor.

FACT

In some countries, people aren't as harmful to the marine environment. They use simple fishing lines and nets to catch enough food to eat and some to sell. Their impact is small.

contaminate make dirty or unfit for use, such as in the pollution or poisoning of an animal or area

Human rubbish is also incredibly harmful to the marine habitat. People often dump plastic items, especially bags and bottles, into the sea. A sea animal may mistake this floating debris for food and eat it. The plastic can choke the animal and cause the animal to suffocate. A sea animal can also get stuck in plastic rings, which chokes the animal or shortens its life.

Fish, such as the Titan triggerfish, will eat plastic rubbish thinking it is food.

Dumping sewage and industrial waste into the marine habitat harms the entire ecosystem. In addition, fish and other marine animals eat such waste and then pass it along the food chain. Remember that the food chain includes humans. This means we could end up eating our own waste! Yuck!

GREAT PACIFIC GARBAGE PATCH

46% OF THE TOTAL MASS IS MADE OF DISCARDED FISHING GEAR

99% OF EVERYTHING IS PLASTIC

1.6 MILLION KM²
994.193 MILLION MILES

1.8 TRILLION PIECES OF PLASTIC

80.000 TONS OF GARBAGE

SAVE THE WORLD
STOP TRASHING OUR OCEAN

San Francisco

8% MICROPLASTICS
13% MESOPLASTICS
26% MACROPLASTICS
53% MEGAPLASTICS

Hawaii

Mexico

GARBAGE CONCENTRATION
Kilograms per square kilometers

0.01   0.1   1   10   100   200 miles

FACT
More than 1 million tons of plastic enters the ocean every year from rivers. The Pacific Ocean contains a floating island of plastic called the Great Pacific Garbage Patch, or GPGP. Located between Hawaii and California, it's the largest mass of ocean plastic in the world. Being made of plastic, it floats rather than sinks. The GPGP covers an area three times the size of France!

THE MARINE HABITAT OF THE FUTURE

The marine habitat has everything humans need to survive. People depend on the marine habitat for food, air and water, and sometimes as a source of income. That's why so many people live near the marine habitat and why it's important to look after it. Examples set by people in Indonesia, Papua New Guinea and New Zealand show ways to live in better harmony with the marine habitat. Countries such as the Philippines have set smaller catch limits and try to avoid catching animals like turtles and young fish. They've created protected areas for marine animals. These examples show that we can still use marine resources respectfully and carefully.

For the marine habitat to survive, problems such as overfishing and polluting need to be addressed. We can protect marine habitats by creating marine reserves and using more environmentally friendly fishing practices. By working together, we can preserve the marine habitat for future generations.

fish farm

WHAT CAN YOU DO?

Consider donating to organizations that protect and preserve the marine habitat. Check tins of seafood and only buy farmed fish. Recycle items that you can and dispose of other rubbish responsibly.

GLOSSARY

aquatic to do with water

bioluminescence production of light by a living organism

contaminate make dirty or unfit for use, such as the pollution or poisoning of an animal or area

coral polyp tiny organism that has a hard limestone skeleton; the skeletons form the structure of coral reefs

crustacean animal with a hard outer skeleton, including crabs, lobsters, crayfish, shrimp and barnacles

ecosystem system of living and non-living things in an environment

erode gradually wear away

estuary mouth of a large river, where the saltwater from an ocean or sea meets fresh water

microorganism tiny organism, usually a bacterium, virus or fungus

migratory having a way of life involving regular travel, such as animals that usually move great distances to find food sources

phytoplankton mainly single-celled plants that live in water and use sunlight and carbon dioxide to make food and oxygen by photosynthesis

sediment sand, mud and other particles produced from weathering

FIND OUT MORE

BOOKS

Endangered Oceans (Endangered Earth), Jody S. Rake
(Raintree, 2019)

Exploring Coral Reefs (Exploring Habitats), Anita Ganeri
(Raintree, 2016)

Marine Biologist (Jobs with Animals), Marne Ventura
(Raintree, 2019)

WEBSITES

bbc.co.uk/bitesize/topics/z849q6f/articles/zmqwscw
Watch this short film to learn more about Earth's five oceans and
some of the threats they face from pollution.

dkfindout.com/uk/earth/oceans-and-seas
Find out more about Earth's oceans and seas, including their
temperature ranges and the flow of their currents.

COMPREHENSION QUESTIONS

1. Why is the marine habitat so important? If humans destroy the marine habitat, what would be the effects on Earth?
2. Name two benefits of coral reefs.
3. What are the five ocean zones? How have plants and animals adapted to live in them?
4. What are some things humans can do to help preserve the marine habitat? What can you do at home to help?

INDEX